DATE DUE

6786

951
W   Willcox, Isobel
           Acrobats & ping pong

ACROBATS
&
PING-PONG

■

Young China's
Games,
Sports,
&
Amusements

■

ACROBATS
&
PING~PONG

Isobel Willcox

Dodd, Mead & Company   New York

Acknowledgments

I owe much to many, to Butler Beaumont, Patricia Bennett, Barbara Brooks, Robert Clogher, Englewood Library staff, Alan Feigenberg, Rose Gevritz, Philip Grushkin, Harry Haines, Mabel Hopper, Henry Hu, Craig Jones, Vera Kalm, Irene Machel, Thomas Masucci, Cepha Pasek, Virginia Payne, Doris Pearsall, Kate Permenter, Kay Ritta, Conrad Schirokauer, Paul Seiz, Ellen Skinner, Janet Smith, David Steinberg, Alfred Sparrow, Joan Tait, Jan Tucker, Oswin Willcox, Betty Williams, Ithmer Wolfe.

Each one contributed help in the making of this book. I gratefully acknowledge my debt to them.

1 2 3 4 5 6 7 8 9 10

Library of Congress Cataloging in Publication Data

Willcox, Isobel.
Acrobats and ping-pong.

Includes index.
SUMMARY: Highlights various forms of recreation enjoyed by the people of China.
1. Sports—China—Juvenile literature. 2. Recreation—China—Juvenile literature. 3. China—Social life and customs—Juvenile literature. [1. Recreation—China. 2. Sports—China. 3. China—Social life and customs] I. Title.
GV651.W54   796′.0951   80-22176
ISBN 0-396-07917-2

CONTENTS

INTRODUCTION

In the year 1912, the vast land of China underwent an important change, one of many changes it has experienced in its long and turbulent history. After centuries of rule by a series of dynasties, headed by emperors, it became a republic. This change came about after a revolutionary uprising led by Dr. Sun Yat-sen, who took over as president.

The ancient Chinese and their early successors had created a remarkable culture. About twelve hundred years ago, China was the most civilized country in the world. She had produced great art and great literature. Her technical men had invented gunpowder, paper manufacture, and printing.

Then Chinese progress slowed. For many centuries the country suffered rebellions and invasions. By the nineteenth century, foreigners controlled some parts of China.

Sun Yat-sen's republic had a short life. Between 1912 and 1949 it was torn by civil wars. Much of the country was divided into two opposing groups, the Nationalists and the Communists. In 1931, Japan seized the northeastern provinces, and in 1937 Japanese armies invaded China proper. The two opposing Chinese groups united against the enemy. But soon after Japan's defeat in World War II, the differences between them widened, and they resumed their war against each other. Chiang Kai-shek tried to hold the Nationalist forces together, but the Communists under Mao Tse-tung were too powerful. In 1934 and 1935, Mao had led his army of 100,000 soldiers westward across China on what is known as the Long March. In 1949, they controlled a large part of the land. Chiang and many of his followers were forced to withdraw to the island of Taiwan. The Communists, led by Mao, set up headquarters in Peking. On October 1, 1949, they proclaimed the founding of the People's Republic of China, with Peking as its capital.

The leaders of the new government made revolutionary changes in Chinese life. One of the most far-reaching changes was the organizing of large groups of towns and villages throughout the country. These organized areas, inhabited mostly by peasants, are called communes. Their directing committees plan and administer the social life, as well as the economic and political activity, of the people. The members of the directing committees are responsible for supervising farm work, running factories, building bridges, settling arguments, paying taxes to the national government, publishing newspapers, and managing small radio stations. They administer schools, housing projects, banks, cemeteries, day care centers, re-forestation plans, stores, libraries, fish ponds, and health centers. In a country devastated by wars, the commune system improved industrial and food production, disease prevention, and the position of women.

Putting great stress on education, the leaders of the People's Republic built thousands of schools. About nine out of ten boys and girls of primary school age now attend classes. Nearly thirty times as many of their older brothers and sisters attend middle school as were enrolled before 1949.

Still another concern of the communes, one to which government leaders at all levels—city, county, provincial, and national—attach great importance, is the recreation of the people. The word "recreation" covers a wide variety of activities, from playing the violin to throwing a beanbag, from making puppets to playing soccer, from watching a movie to building a model ship.

Why do the government leaders think that leisure activities are important for children and adults? When this vast country must work hard to feed, clothe, house, and provide medical care for a billion people, why does it devote resources and effort to putting on plays and track meets, building libraries and swimming pools, offering art and Ping-Pong lessons? Here is how one Chinese writer answers.

Discussing the value of sports, he says: "Taking part in a wide range of sports improves the people's physical fitness and promotes industrial and agricultural production. It gives the people added vigor to build our country." In addition, he points out that athletes who participate in international sports events promote friendship and exchange experiences with people of other countries.

Art, music, and books contribute in other ways:

—They help to keep alive the great heritage of China's ancient past.

—They effectively express ideas that the leaders want the children and adults to remember.

—They offer enjoyment and relaxation when the people are not working or studying.

Such benefits and satisfactions, the leaders say, enrich the lives of the Chinese from nursery school years to old age. Because the people are better able to build and develop the country, the effort and resources invested in recreation are amply justified.

Until 1976, the ideas that the leaders wanted the people to remember were chiefly those of Chairman Mao. Since his death and the political unrest that followed, the new ruling group has modified the Maoist policies on education, culture, and industry. It has also sought closer ties with non-Communist countries.

Another change the new leaders have made is the adoption of a new system of spelling Chinese words with the Roman alphabet. The new system, called Pinyin, for the Chinese word meaning "transcription," has been adopted by the United Nations and by the United States Board on Geographic Names. It helps Westerners come closer to the proper pronunciation of Chinese names. Tientsin, for instance, is now spelled Tianjin. The spelling for Shantung is Shandong, and Nanking is now Nanjing. Mao Tse-tung's name becomes Mao Zedong, and Deputy Prime Minister Teng Hsiaso-ping's name is now Deng Xiaoping.

A few exceptions are made for words so commonly used in English that a change in spelling would be confusing. Peking, Canton, Inner Mongolia, Tibet, and Yangtse River are examples of such exceptions.

Pinyin spelling for place names and proper names has been used in this book. To aid the reader in identifying the new spellings with their former versions, a glossary is appended at the end of the book.

THE PEOPLE'S REPUBLIC OF CHINA

SOVIET UNION

ALTAI

MTS

M O N

Xinjiang

AFGHANISTAN

PAKISTAN

Qinghai

C

H

Xizang
(Tibet)

HIMALAYA MTS.

NEPAL

Lhasa ●

S
(Sz

BHUTAN

INDIA

BANGLADESH

Kur

Yu

BURMA

Bay of Bengal

THAILAND

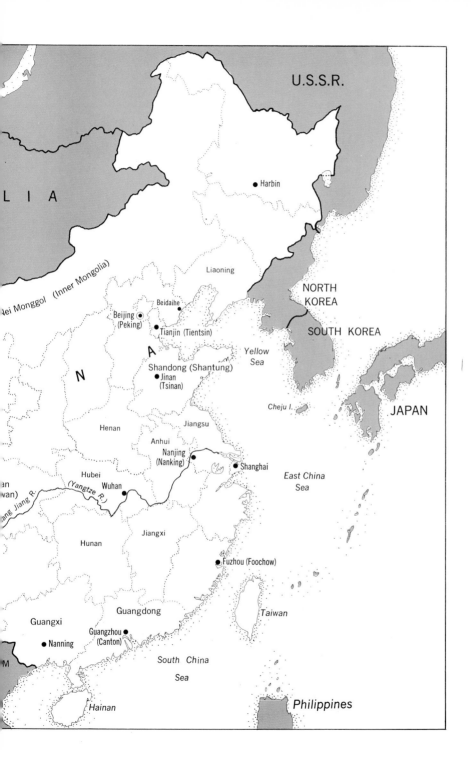

U.S.S.R.

● Harbin

L I A

Nei Monggol (Inner Mongolia)

Liaoning

NORTH
KOREA

Beidaihe

Beijing ◉
(Peking)

● Tianjin (Tientsin)

SOUTH KOREA

A

Yellow
Sea

N

Shandong (Shantung)
● Jinan
(Tsinan)

Cheju I.

JAPAN

Henan

Jiangsu

Anhui

Nanjing
(Nanking)

● Shanghai

East China
Sea

Hubei

(Yangtze R.)
Wuhan ●

an)
van)

ang Jiang R.

Jiangxi

Hunan

● Fuzhou (Foochow)

Taiwan

Guangdong

Guangxi

Guangzhou ●
(Canton)

● Nanning

South China

Sea

M

Hainan

Philippines

1

■

CARTWHEELS
&
BALANCE BEAMS

School playgrounds in Shanghai, the largest city in the People's Republic of China, are busy places. Every day in good weather classes take turns going outside for games and exercise. Usually, four or five classes share a playground at the same time. One class may run relay races while another shoots baskets. Some classes play volleyball while others practice gymnastics, one of the most popular sports in China.

Coaches and teachers help the students develop skills on balance beams and parallel bars. They lead them in calisthenics and teach them stunts like somersaults and cartwheels.

Middle school students in Shanghai enjoy gymnastics and basket shooting.

Today a group of teachers on tour from the United
States is visiting a girls' class in a gymnasium in Peking.
One of the visitors is struck immediately by the elegant
posture of the girls.

"How well they hold themselves," she says, "and how
beautifully they walk."

She asks the tour guide whether most Chinese girls
have such well-proportioned bodies and carry themselves
so well.

"Our Chinese children are generally in good physical

A gymnastics teacher in Peking helps a student demonstrate a hand position.

condition," says the genial guide, "but these girls are a special group. I'll let their teacher tell you about them."

"Yes," explains the teacher, "these girls were chosen from all over the city and from nearby farms to receive extra training in gymnastics."

"How did you select them?" asks another of the visitors.

"When they were in kindergarten and the early grades, their teachers noticed that they were talented. They were well built, and they were the best runners. Their coordi-

Young people learn about gymnastics as they watch a champion vaulter in the Jinan Stadium.

nation was good, and they learned the folk dances better than their classmates did. Their teachers recommended them for this special school. Some of us went to observe them, and we chose the best."

The teacher adds that the girls' talents are not enough to qualify them for special training. It is important, too, for a girl to have a strong desire to be a good gymnast. She must also be willing to work hard at mastering the skills and to share them with other people.

From the time when they were preschool toddlers, these girls, like all children in China, have been taught that it is their duty to help others. SERVE THE PEOPLE, say the posters, books, banners, songs, and radio programs in every village, town, and city.

So these girls—and the talented boys who are similarly chosen—know that the extra training they receive carries with it several obligations. As soon as they are ready, they will be expected to entertain the farm workers with

their stunts. They will help rural teachers train students in regular physical education classes. In the gyms and auditoriums of factory workers' apartment houses these specially trained girls and boys will put on gymnastics exhibitions. They will also give performances for soldiers at army posts.

A thousand and more at a time, they will put on demonstrations in huge stadiums to mark holidays and festive

This talented five-year-old is taking part in a gymnastics exhibition in Peking.

occasions. Audiences applaud these performances enthusiastically.

Audiences also respond with delight to exhibitions by students who are training to be acrobats. These young people are selected in the same way the gymnasts are chosen. They go to schools that specialize in acrobatics.

This kind of entertainment has a long history in China. Two thousand years ago acrobats entertained audiences with their acts.

Nowadays nearly every town and city and commune has at least one acrobatic troupe. Starting with somersaults and cartwheels, which all children like to do, the most able boys and girls go on to feats requiring skilled balancing and faultless timing. Before long they are performing more difficult acts. What a thrill it is for a boy when he can hop onto a moving bicycle with eight other acrobats already on it! And how proud he is when he can then do stunts on another boy's shoulders as the bicycle

Rural children in Anhui Province have joined a group of peasants to learn techniques of weight lifting. The instructor is using homemade equipment.

takes its crew of nine around a gym or across a stage.

An acrobat soon learns, too, to bounce a ball off the top of his head as he takes a solo ride on a one-wheeled cycle ten feet tall. Acrobats help each other learn to do stunts like balancing a plate on the top of a long pole and dancing as they twirl it.

Like the gymnasts, the acrobats share their skills with others. They go to rural areas where there are no special coaches. They train the young people there, and when the rural groups cannot buy sports equipment, the visiting athletes help them make it themselves.

The leaders of the Chinese people are proud of the acrobats. In 1978 they sent one of their best acrobatic troupes to the United States to entertain American audiences in theaters and to express friendship for the American people. The acrobats were invited to appear on television in this country. Millions of Americans marveled at their feats.

2

■

POOLS
&
BEACHES

Like American children, Chinese girls and boys love to swim. In southern China, where it is always warm, they can go swimming all year round. In the northern provinces they have about two months of swimming weather.

Many towns and cities have built swimming pools. The children flock to them. They splash and duck and try the strokes their coaches have been teaching them. Even very young ones take swimming lessons. In some places they are expected to swim several hundred meters in four different styles.

The leaders of China know that games and exercise help keep the children and adults in good physical condi-

tion. They want the people to be strong and healthy, so that they can accomplish the enormous tasks that lie ahead for China. Everyone, they say, must work hard to bring the country up to date in agriculture, science, technology, and defense by the year 2000. This is an ambitious goal. So they make plans for many kinds of play, exercise, and games. They encourage the schools, the

This new tile-bordered pool for children is connected with a municipal sports stadium in Shanghai. Coaches at such pools conduct classes for schoolchildren, including those in nursery school.

communes, the factories, and the city neighborhoods to carry out the plans.

Teachers and coaches hold frequent meetings with leaders in their areas to discuss the sports activities they will supervise.

"A game on a playground is not just a game," says one of the leaders at such a meeting. "It is also an occasion

Children at a summer day camp put their best effort into a tug-of-war contest.

for learning to be a better person. We think that children in a swimming pool can learn more than swimming."

"For example," says another leader, "an older boy learns about serving the people when he helps a younger one improve his backstroke. And a young girl learns the value of working together when she helps her team win a tug-of-war game. Sports can help children develop good character traits."

Leaders, teachers, and coaches all over China firmly believe in this method of conducting sports activities. It is the method they follow when they direct games, swimming lessons, gymnastics, and other sports. They hope that the children will put the character traits to good use in their schools and neighborhoods and, later on, in their work places.

Some high school students in Nanjing put their self-reliance and cooperative spirit to good use not long ago.

Farm girls in Guangdong Province swim in one of the rivers that criss-cross their commune.

This is what they did:

There was no swimming pool at their school. They wanted very much to have one. After talking with the school principal about it, they saw that they could have a pool if they built it themselves. They knew that it would be a difficult job, but they set to work eagerly. Men who knew about building pools gave them advice. Now

Swimming is one of the summer camp activities at Beidaihe, a famous beach resort.

the students proudly show visitors the pool they built.

Children who live outside the cities swim in lakes and rivers and in the ocean. Like the specially trained gymnasts, students who are chosen for intensive swimming courses have an obligation to help the children on the farms. Each year many of them go out to the countryside to teach the rural children to be good swimmers.

3

■

INDOORS
&
OUTDOORS

Millions of young people in China are learning to be good runners, good jumpers, good Ping-Pong players, and good sports. They learn these things in their gyms and on their playgrounds and sports fields.

Jump rope is a favorite game in China. Just as in the United States, it is more popular among girls than it is among boys.

In addition to the usual style of jumping with one rope at a time, some girls have mastered a much more difficult way. They turn a small rope themselves and do jumps over that while they jump over a long rope turned by two other girls.

A ten-year-old girl in Nanjing drew this picture of children on her school playground. They are playing Ping-Pong, jumping rope, and shooting baskets. She said she was the girl who tripped on the rope.

Chanting rhymes to keep time is part of the fun in Tianjin, as it is wherever children jump rope.

This game was played in China two thousand years ago.

Beginning with their earliest years in nursery school, girls and boys enjoy playground activities.

Since almost every woman in China except the very old works outside her home, the families must arrange care for their youngest children during the day. Many city mothers, when they leave for work, take them on their bicycles and drop them off at a nursery school. The committees which manage the factories and offices where the mothers work often provide nursery schools in one section of their buildings.

Each nursery school has an outside area, sometimes bordered by trees and shrubs, where the children play with balls and hoops and run relay races. They enjoy playground equipment such as swings, slides, rocking boats, seesaws, and carousels. They learn to climb, to throw, to balance, and to hop.

The lessons in helping others begin early. Two- and

three-year-olds are taught to take turns in playing on the
equipment and not to litter their playgrounds. They
learn that they must not grab a ball or a toy from some-
one who is using it.

At first, when the children reach kindergarten, they
play on the same kinds of equipment that nursery school
children use. Then, guided by their teachers, they soon
take up activities that require greater skill. Most kindergarten children play tag. Many of them learn to play

Young children use their nursery school equipment during an outdoor play period.

A nursery school boy and his younger brother try a slide for the first time. They are not yet sure they like it.

shuttlecock. Climbing ropes and high poles attracts some, especially boys.

How skillfully a five-year-old pole climber does his stunt: Gripping the fifteen-foot pole with his arms and legs, he inches his way to the top. From there he looks down to see who has been watching him. He flings one arm up in the gesture of an experienced performer and waits for a sign of approval. Then he loosens his grip and slides quickly to the ground.

When these boys and girls move up to elementary school, they add games that demand still more skill. They

In her spick-and-span pinafore, this girl takes a ride on a carou-
sel. Her school is on a farm commune.

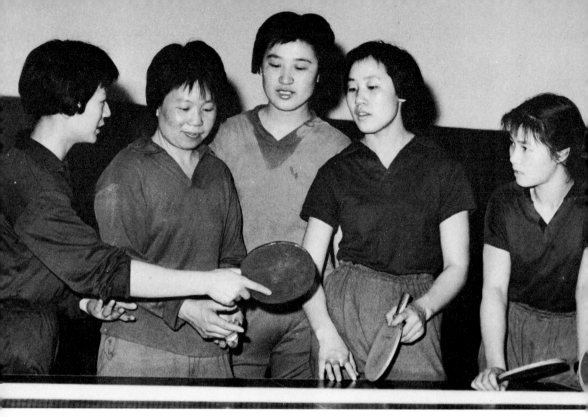

throw rubber darts at target boards and play badminton. In these grades they begin gymnastics and acrobatics.

Older children go on to marathons, bicycle races, softball, and other sports that are familiar to American high school students: volleyball, ice hockey, field hockey, and track and field.

Soccer is one of the most popular games in the People's Republic. A single county in southern China has 240 fields where its more than two thousand soccer teams play. Enthusiastic spectators crowd into stadiums to watch soccer games. They pay about thirty cents admission.

The most widespread popular game in China is Ping-Pong, or table tennis. It requires little space. The equip-

A Ping-Pong player in Sichuan shares pointers on the game with other girls. Most Chinese players hold their paddles with a pen-hold grip.

ment is not expensive. Schools, commune halls, factories, and recreation centers can afford it. Children as young as four years learn to play Ping-Pong. They use mini-paddles and play on small tables. Thousands of them become excellent players. Visiting Americans have watched in amazement the blazing serves and the brilliant returns of eleven-year-old girls.

In some towns and cities teachers select the best young players. Buses then pick up these children five afternoons a week and take them to clubs or recreation centers for extra coaching in the game. To make up for the school lessons they miss, they go to evening school twice a week.

During the 1950s Ping-Pong players had many discussions about the best way to hold the paddle. Some argued in favor of the pen-hold grip. Others said that the tennis-style grip was better. Then, in 1952, a Japanese Ping-Pong team, using the pen-hold grip, won a tourna-

These young Ping-Pong players are intently watching older children play the game in a Peking gymnasium.

ment against the leading Chinese team. Many Chinese players switched to the pen-hold grip. Now most good players in China describe their game as a close-to-the-table, fast attack, with the pen-hold grip.

In 1971, as one of the first friendly exchanges between the United States and the People's Republic, a team of American Ping-Pong players was invited to China. They played a series of matches with the best Chinese players. The Chinese team won the series.

Ping-Pong is usually played by one player against one other. In contrast, relay races—also popular in China—pit a team of runners against another team. Each person's effort counts toward his team's success.

A slogan quoted over and over in China says: "Cooperation first, competition second." Another slogan expresses the idea this way: "Friendship first, competition second."

Teachers often talk to their pupils about cooperation. "It is important," they say, "for us to learn to play and work together. People on our farms and in our factories and mines must cooperate if we are to build a prosperous country."

Coaches and their teams of older students also talk about friendship and competition. The captain of a Peking University basketball team and a Canadian student who was taking part in sports there recently discussed these ideas.

"Winning takes second place with us," the captain

said. "We get our satisfaction from knowing that we have played our best and from trying to raise the level of athletic performance. Competitors should not get carried away in their desire to win. We are taught that."

The Canadian had earlier observed an incident that illustrates how the Chinese put these ideas into practice. He described it to some of his American friends. "First," he said, "you should know that the Chinese really love

Middle school basketball players leave the court after a practice session.

Cooperation and competition are combined in relay races like this one.

basketball. Every school and commune has a court. Every factory and neighborhood that has space builds one or at least puts up a basket. The Chinese play the game faster than we do, and they *do* like to win, of course. But here is what I saw. In the middle of an important tournament game a player slipped and fell down. A player on the other team gave up a fast break to help him get up. I've heard of other incidents like that."

33

4

■

MEETS
&
RALLIES

Crack! The starter's gun goes off. Six lean runners sprint down the track. They are competing in the 100-yard dash. It is one of the events at the National Games being held on this crisp autumn day.

As many as seven thousand young athletes are taking part in this field day. They are competing in such events as hurdle races, swimming, discus throwing, pole vaulting, and the high jump.

The Workers Stadium in Peking is the setting for the National Games, which are held every four years. Thousands of people fill the stands of the huge arena. They have come to see not only the sports events but also the

Boys taking part in the National Games get a fast start in the
100-yard dash.

breathtaking displays staged by the athletes. Colorful
opening ceremonies feature bands, banners, massed flags,
and "march-ins" by the participants.

Some of the sports events are spectacular and entertaining in themselves, such as a demonstration of calisthenics performed by 25,000 people dressed in bright
costumes.

Schoolchildren are among the spectators who applaud this pole vaulter after he completes his jump.

Girls attending a meet in Peking watch a performer on the high swing.

Other brilliant events take the form of pageants. They dramatize such themes as growing up sturdy, the benefits of recent political changes, honor to the Red flag, and pride in the technology at a large petroleum plant. Enormous painted scenic backgrounds add to the excitement of the skillfully staged performances.

(Above) Six hundred Young Pioneers make their entry at the National Games. As members of a patriotic youth group, they pledge to do good deeds for others and for their country.

(Left) A colorful "march-in" opens the National Games in the Workers Stadium in Peking.

Hundreds of white-shirted students join arms in a calisthenics display titled "Ode to the Red Flag."

Along with the National Games, tournaments held in other cities build a spirit of unity among the Chinese people. They also strengthen the determination to help China achieve its goal of becoming a modernized country.

Like other stadiums in China, the Peking arena has a library built into it. The library specializes in books on physical fitness and health care. Like stadiums in the United States, those in China have public address systems. Unlike announcers at American stadiums, however, the Chinese announcers are actually teachers. Using loudspeakers, the announcer teaches the spectators about the sport they are watching.

"We are here to learn," he says at the beginning of an event. Then he gives the rules that govern the sport. He wants the spectators to learn to recognize the moves of a good wrestler and the techniques of a good pole vaulter.

Gymnasts form a spectacular design of flower petals and dragon figures to celebrate China's national holiday on October 1 in honor of the founding of the People's Republic.

He points out such moves and techniques. That helps to improve the spectators' own performances and raises the level of the game everywhere.

A typical Chinese crowd's reactions during a game seem unusual to American visitors. The Chinese do not usually root for just one side. They clap equally for skillful plays by members of both teams, even at international meets. This is part of their code of sportsmanship.

When an announcer notes a special act of fair play, he shares it with the spectators. Not long ago, for example, the announcer at a girls' volleyball game broadcast that a player had admitted having broken the rule against touching the net. The referee had not seen her

error and was letting the game go on. The girl herself reported it to him and was penalized. The crowd applauded her for her good sportsmanship.

Competing players are expected to be courteous to each other. Sometimes before a game the teams line up and, raising their hands, call out, "We will learn from our opponents." The home team offers tea and clean towels to its visitors.

The athletes at the National Games have worked hard for the honor of competing here. First, they were chosen to attend one of about a thousand sports schools in China. These Physical Training Institutes and Youth

43

Amateur Athletic Schools take children aged seven through sixteen after school three times a week. Coaches there put them through a rigorous training. These schools are the sources of China's sports champions and physical education teachers.

Stadiums throughout the People's Republic of China are the setting also for rallies and sports exhibitions. At these events the young people do not compete. They display their skills.

Even nursery school children take part in exhibitions.

"Blazing a New Trail" is the title of this scene in a calisthenics pageant. It marks China's change of political leaders in 1976 after the death of Mao Zedong.

One of the events they like is the tricycle parade. They dress up for it and sometimes decorate the tricycles with paper flowers.

Neither their school nor their parents give them the flowers. How, then, do three-year-olds get them? They buy them with money they earn.

How can three-year-olds earn money? Here is one answer, a uniquely Chinese way, which a group of foreign visitors discovered at a flashlight factory.

This factory employs many women. Next to it is a nursery school which cares for their small children during working hours. As in all Chinese schools, the course of study includes at least one period a week of practical work. This is considered a subject just like arithmetic, language, and music.

The leaders of China think that everyone should learn about factory work and farming, even if he or she is not

45

刻苦鍛练·增强体质·攀登世界体育高峰!

(Above) Little gymnasts form pyramids at a sports exhibition in Peking.

(Left) High school students do a balancing stunt at the National Games.

going to be a worker or a farmer. It is good, they say, for scientists and secretaries and singers to understand and respect manual labor, and the best way to do that is to be a farmer or a worker for a while.

Each school from nursery to university is paired with a factory or a farm. The managers select for each class one or more safe and suitable steps in the work for the students to take part in.

Nursery school children in Henan ride decorated tricycles at a sports exhibition.

They send money to the school to pay for this work. Instead of dividing it up among the students, the teacher puts it into a class account. When young children need it for decorations or for dance and play costumes, they draw it from their account.

At the flashlight factory the managers chose a safe, easy job for the three-year-olds. The youngsters drop tiny flashlight bulbs into cardboard shipping cartons.

So these children had three reasons to feel proud when they rode their tricycles at the exhibition. They were proud of riding well in the parade. They were proud that

As many as ten thousand people come to sing in this rally in northeast China. Music students from their schools accompany them.

they had earned the money for the flowers. Their teachers had praised them for their work, which helped their country, and they were proud of that, too.

Their older brothers and sisters have more difficult jobs in their work periods. They spend the money they earn on such things as educational films and sports equipment.

Sports meets and exhibitions are not the only big events which the Chinese stage in their stadiums. They also hold cultural rallies. At some of these gatherings several thousand boys and girls join together to sing. They are members of music groups at their schools and recreation centers. The rallies are held to mark a national anniversary or an important occasion like the opening of a new bridge.

At other cultural rallies large crowds attend to see troupes of amateur and professional entertainers. These troupes dance, put on plays, and sing.

5

■

AUDIENCES
&
PERFORMERS

The beating of drums and the sound of flutes are coming from a large tent pitched in a meadow where yaks and sheep are grazing. Several children are looking through the tent opening. They see drummers and flute players sitting on a brightly colored felt rug. An old man is dancing. He performs the steps and gestures with great dignity. Gradually other old men come forward to dance. Men and women stand in a half-circle to watch. The children are surprised to see a foreigner among them.

The musicians, the dancers, and all of the audience except the foreigner and his interpreter are Tadzhiks who live in the western part of China. They have left their animals in the meadow and are welcoming the foreigner. He is an American newspaperman who has traveled more than two thousand miles from Peking and climbed to this ten-thousand-foot-high meadow to see how the Tadzhiks live.

He is fascinated by the flute players as they produce piping sounds on their bone flutes. He watches with great interest as the drummers tap the drums with their fingers. The performance of these men is probably very much like the welcome their ancestors gave to Marco Polo when he passed through this land seven hundred years ago.

As the visitor and his interpreter drive on to their next stop, they talk about dances of farmers and herders.

"In many rural areas," says the interpreter, "only the old people know the steps of the dances now."

"Does that mean that these kinds of dances will die out?" asks the American.

Dancers do a folk dance to entertain peasants who have been har-
vesting corn.

An old woman on Hainan Island teaches an arts troupe a dance which she performed many years ago.

"In some cases, yes," says the interpreter. He explains that to preserve these dances before they all disappear, troupes of professional entertainers visit farming and herding settlements. The old men and women there teach them the dances and the music they remember from their youth. Then the troupes include them in the programs they give for audiences in other communes and in the towns and cities.

Children in other parts of China learn them, sometimes in simplified versions, and perform them for each other and for visitors.

China has inherited from the past a rich tradition in the performing arts. Much of it is being preserved. Chinese operas, with their singers, dancers, and acrobats, are exciting musical events today.

What makes old Chinese operas exciting? The costumes are vivid and elaborate, the plots are engrossing.

The make-up exaggerates the evil of the villains. The good men fight the bad men and win.

Cymbals, drums, and gongs mark the high points of the action with loud crashing sounds. Flutes and stringed instruments accompany the other parts. Kings, warriors, and princesses are among the characters in operas based on historical tales, old folk stories, and legends.

China's old folk songs are kept alive by schoolchildren and by entertainers, both professional and amateur. The

singing of old (and new) songs is a feature of many entertainments and ceremonies.

In a Peking park, strollers are pleased when they come upon a chorus of schoolchildren. Led by one of their classmates, they are giving an informal concert for the people who have come to see the flowers and the palaces.

Soloists and choruses perform at meetings and at holi-

(Above) Like other talented children, this little dancer has been singled out for special lessons.

(Left) A school playground is the stage for these young dancers.

day celebrations. Observing the Chinese respect for the elderly, singing groups visit retirement homes to entertain old people who have no families.

Puppetry is also an art that has passed from generation to generation for centuries. Puppet shows in parks and recreation centers carry on this traditional kind of theater.

Storytelling, another popular form of entertainment,

goes far, far back to the time when few people could read
and write. Well-loved stories passed orally from parents
to children. Almost everyone in China can read now, but
storytelling still flourishes. Today storytellers gather
audiences in teahouses, neighborhood courtyards, and
parks. Women and older children, as well as men, tell
stories.

Many an evening in a village a storyteller sets up a
table or a panel of rough illustrations in front of the commune hall. This immediately attracts an audience. The
storyteller has a gift for narrating a story in a dramatic
way. Characters in adventure stories and old tales come
alive as he recounts their deeds. Occasionally he points

A soloist and chorus, accompanied on Western instruments, sing a song in praise of education for working people.

to the illustrations to help his listeners follow the plot.

Tickets for entertainments in theaters are priced to fit Chinese budgets. Admission to new films costs about twenty-two cents, to old films seventeen cents. Students pay five cents.

It doesn't often happen in China that an opera is just an exciting spectacle or a puppet show just an amusing little play. The leaders of the country expect entertainment to express ideas which they want people to think about. So performances usually entertain and teach at the same time.

Here are a few examples of how this is done:

—An old play that keeps children in a happy state of suspense also tells them about unfair judges of the past.

—A clever monkey in an old opera, *The Monkey King*, outwits villains whose actions seem to resemble those of today's political men now out of favor.

A storyteller narrates incidents from a popular novel. The sign gives the name of the book, *All Men Are Brothers*.

The red scarfs these children are wearing show that they are Young Pioneers. They are singing a song to teach a political lesson.

—Boys and girls are doubled up with laughter at a modern comedy skit while they are learning that some of their ideas about illness are mere superstitions.

—Typical characters in modern operas are men and women soldiers who conquered China's enemies and shepherd girls who risked their lives in a blizzard to save the commune's sheep.

—Storytellers' themes include catching spies and praise for model communes.

—Sometimes an old man tells a true "before-and-after" story. He describes the terrible conditions in the coal mines when he was young. Or he recounts the hardship of the Long March, a famous wartime event of 1934–1935.

In 1976, when Chairman Mao Zedong died, new leaders took office at the head of the government. They began gradually to say that sometimes shows which emphasized teaching were rather heavy-handed and—some thought

Children listen eagerly to an old man tell about his commune's early struggles.

—even boring. Now entertainment is not always so plainly educational as it was. But most of it still contains a lesson. A rollicking new popular song for older children and adults says that everyone wants to get a washing machine so that China will catch up with the modern countries. It is done in a spirit of fun, but the double purpose—entertaining and teaching—is clear.

Ideas about political men and model communes are minor elements in variety shows. The programs for such shows include pantomimers, singers, dancers, acrobats, jugglers, magicians, and men who imitate bird calls, locomotive sounds, and the crashing of bombs.

The applause is loud and enthusiastic for acts in which an animal trainer puts a panda through a series of stunts. This lumbering, lovable animal, native to Tibet, looks like a bear but is related to the raccoon. People watch in amazement when a trained panda responds to instruc-

tions to climb onto a stool, to mount a slide, and to roll a barrel.

Such an act is pure entertainment. But even the light-hearted variety show sometimes finds ways to express an important idea. A love song about a young woman and a rose illustrates one such way.

A Chinese ensemble performs a Japanese folk dance.

Love songs, which until about 1979 were not included in entertainment in the People's Republic, made their appearance indirectly at first. "To which young man shall I give this rose?" sings the young woman. She wonders which is the most admirable of the three she is considering. When she decides to give the flower to the third one—the scientist—it is clear that the song is not really a love song. It is a way of giving prestige to scientists. For some time peasants, workers, and soldiers have been featured in songs. Now, in its push toward modernization,

China wants more scientists. So they are the heroes of some of the new songs.

Chinese films, radio, and television share the two-fold aim of teaching and entertaining. They share, too, the current trend toward a lighter touch in presenting ideas about serving the people and modernizing the country.

The subjects of movies range from the Chinese Revolution to science, from the lives of important men and women to travel, from disagreements among shipyard workers to building a railroad in East Africa. Chinese

Audiences like the acrobats' acts in variety shows.

movie producers also make comedies, dramatic pictures, and musical films.

On television, children can see cartoons, sports, news programs, and special events like the 1979 visit of Deputy Prime Minister Deng Xiaoping to the United States. Some crime stories and family comedies are shown on Chinese television and movie screens. Love stories, in which the lovers are timid and demure, began to appear about 1979.

Few families have television sets of their own. Most children who see television watch it in groups at clubrooms and community halls in their neighborhoods and apartment houses. Some schools and communes also have television sets for group viewing.

Nearly every home in China, however, has a radio. In addition, programs can be heard in city squares, in schools, and in fields. Radio stations broadcast entertainment, news, weather, music, speeches, and announce-

ments. Special programs for children offer games, songs, stories, and lessons in health, history, and science.

China has recently opened its doors to selected entertainment from abroad. Chinese children like Charlie Chaplin pictures from the United States. Long lines form outside movie theaters showing European and American films like *The Hunchback of Notre Dame, Hamlet, Convoy,* and cowboy pictures.

Since 1976 foreign programs have been added to the Chinese television schedule. On television as well as in

(Left) Children like to watch a panda do a trick like this.

(Right) A trainer in a Nanjing variety show puts a panda through his stunts.

auditoriums, people now enjoy American symphony orchestras, European musical groups, and Japanese dance companies.

They also see Chinese companies performing ballets based on European ballet movements. These companies do serious ballets with revolutionary themes and also fanciful ballets. From Denmark comes the tender story by Hans Christian Andersen which is told in the ballet *The Little Match Girl*.

Imported, too, though only in small numbers, are Japanese cassette recorders and Hong Kong cassettes with

American pop tunes and country-and-western music.

Chinese sailors sometimes buy goods for their families when their ships stop at Hong Kong and at Yokahama, Japan. That is how some households in port cities like Shanghai and Tianjin have obtained television sets of their own.

After having been forbidden for many years by the country's leaders, ballroom dancing was revived in 1979. Older middle school students now can attend dances sponsored—and strictly supervised—by their schools. No rock 'n' roll is permitted.

The trainer scrubs the panda between stage performances.

Four-fifths of China's population—nearly eight hundred million people—are agricultural workers. The leaders of the country want them to enjoy and to learn from plays, films, and variety shows just as city people do.

Nearly eight hundred million people! It is a gigantic task to send entertainment to them, but more and more children in rural China are seeing actors and hearing singers from the cities.

How is this accomplished? In the clubhouse of a Shandong village is one answer to that question. A troupe of variety show performers from a city has traveled to this rural area—as gifted acrobats and swimmers do—and is putting on a show. In addition, its members are teaching farm youths some of their acts, so that they, in turn, can entertain other country people.

Similarly, acting companies take their plays to the country. The heroes and heroines in some of these plays

A Japanese ballet troupe rehearses the archery dance of a ballet it is presenting in Chinese cities.

This farm girl has been honored as a volunteer who organized art programs in her village. Here she is practicing a song. The poster behind her says: "Literature guides the peasants, workers, and soldiers."

are rural men, women, and children who struggled thirty years ago to change bare, rocky hillsides into orchards.

Projection crews take films to remote areas which few traveling performers have yet reached. They show films and train young people to run the projectors. They then arrange to lend them films.

Some units of the People's Liberation Army which are stationed at posts far from towns and cities do their part. The soldiers learn folk dances and songs, so that they can entertain the herding and farming families near their bases.

Finally, radio reaches out to the rural people, carrying information and leisure-time fun. Out in the country some communes have small radio stations. The people put on songs and skits they write themselves. Local musicians, too, give concerts on these stations. They often play instruments like those their ancestors played centuries ago.

6

WUSHU
&
BIBA

Seven hundred years ago Chinese people were doing *wushu*, a form of exercise that is still popular today.

The English term for *wushu* is "martial arts." This name can be misleading. An early morning visit to a city park shows why.

What a sight this is! Dozens and dozens of men and women, some in their seventies, are out here. Grouped at random among the trees, they are doing exercises.

How gently they move! Their arms glide up, down, forward, around. Sometimes they seem to be doing a slow dance.

These movements were once part of a series of martial

Children do *wushu* on a playground.

self-defense measures. Martial means "warlike." Today *wushu* (also called shadowboxing) has nothing to do with fighting.

Why do so many people, young and old, like to do these exercises?

For relaxation, some say.

To keep physically fit, say others.

To feel in harmony with nature, say some of the older people.

The Chinese word for this particular type of *wushu* is

dai ji-quan. It is a system of 128 movements. Many people who do *dai ji-quan* limit themselves to 38 movements.

Another type of *wushu* is called *gong-fu.* Its movments are more rigid than those of *dai ji-quan.* Still another form of *wushu* features wooden swords and lances and bamboo spears. Its movements are precise and formal. They require great skill and lightning-fast reactions. Audiences at exhibitions of this sport like the traditional red-and-white costumes and the red-tasseled swords.

In recent years these sports have attracted a following

These youngsters are practicing one of the martial arts.

in the United States. Both children and adults in this country are enrolled in classes organized by *wushu* instructors.

LEARN FROM THE PAST is an often-repeated motto in China. The centuries-old sports are one example of what the Chinese learn from their past.

They have, of course, discarded many of the old ways of doing things. Beginning in 1949, when the People's Republic of China was founded, they have eliminated famines and epidemics of contagious diseases. Instead of letting the rivers flood their fields, as often happened, they build flood control projects. They no longer cripple women's feet by binding them for years in tight bandages.

But, heeding the motto, they keep good things that flourished in the past. One such good thing is the maintenance of strong ties among parents and children and

83

A boy playing an *erhu* accompanies a trio of singers in traditional costumes.

their relatives. Another is respect for old people. Traditional music is one more of the good things from past centuries that the Chinese are preserving.

The old music is played on instruments that were designed hundreds of years ago. One of them, the *gujin*, is a two-stringed instrument that resembles a violin. The *biba*, also a stringed instrument, is plucked, like a banjo. Other traditional instruments are the *sheng*, a mouth organ, and the bamboo flute.

Children who take lessons on such instruments need

not buy their own. They can borrow them to practice on after school.

Chinese children also take lessons on Western musical instruments. Thousands of them are learning to play the piano, the cello, the cornet, the clarinet, and other instruments that American children play. They learn to play them at music schools and at recreation centers called Children's Palaces. These centers offer many other kinds of recreation, from sports to crafts.

(Above) a performer in a variety show plays a solo on the *biba*.

(Right) This worker in a musical instrument factory is tuning a *galong jin*. Hanging on the wall are several other traditional instruments.

7

■

HOBBIES
&
AMUSEMENTS

The stirring sounds of "The East Is Red" ring out. A children's glee club is singing the Chinese national song. The scene is a room in a Children's Palace in Shanghai. These boys and girls have come together to sing folk songs and songs about a good teacher, a river in China, and enemies of the people.

This Children's Palace is one of many recreation centers located in various sections of the city. It is a large building several stories high. Before 1949 it was the home of an Englishman who carried on business in Shanghai. Now it belongs to the city. In some of its dozens of rooms children sing, play in an orchestra, take

A glee club member takes a turn conducting in a Children's Palace in Shanghai.

music lessons, and practice on the instruments they are learning to play.

Talented pupils from elementary and middle schools come here for after-school activities. Most other cities in China have recreation centers like this. As in Shanghai, the children can choose from a long list of hobbies and amusements.

In a Children's Palace in Nanjing, a hall is equipped for China's favorite sport, Ping-Pong. The *toc toc* of fast-bouncing balls is the only sound in the room as pairs of children concentrate on their game. In nearby rooms children who like to dance are doing folk dances and ballet.

Outdoors in a play area two teams of boys are playing volleyball. One boy's grandfather, who used to be a peas-

Among the many activities at this Children's Palace, Ping-Pong is the choice of these children.

ant and is now retired, has walked over from his house to watch. During the game he turns to another old man who is watching and says,

"When I was a boy we didn't know what a ball game was. Our days were all work. No school. No play. I never held a ball in my hand until my son was growing up. Those were bitter days. Our grandchildren have a much better life now." The other old man nods in agreement.

Millions of children of the old man's generation grew up not knowing what a box of crayons or a paint box was. Here, in this Children's Palace in Nanjing, rooms for arts and crafts occupy a whole floor. The old man has marveled at the pictures his grandchildren bring home from art classes at school and at the Children's Palace.

What kinds of handwork are the children doing here? Building model planes? Painting? Making ship models? Yes, they enjoy these hobbies just as American children do. The girls and boys in the pottery class are shaping

Girls and boys make ship models in an after-school recreation center.

colorful bowls and plates. Their teacher is a retired potter who comes to share his skills with them.

An elderly woman in another room is passing on skills she learned fifty years ago. She is helping children with their needlework projects.

Typically Chinese are the crafts chosen by the children who are working in other rooms on this floor. One group is cutting out paper designs like those which the Chinese mount on windows, walls, and doors for New Year's Day. Some younger boys and girls are also work-

A boy shows visitors in a Children's Palace the model plane he is building.

ing with scissors and bright-colored paper. Carrying on an ancient Chinese tradition, they are making three-dimensional birds in imaginative shapes.

Traditional, too, is the artwork which ten or twelve children are doing with brushes. The designs on their kites and fans have the flavor of very old Chinese art.

Also centuries old is the style of brushwork in the calligraphy class. Calligraphy is the art of doing elegant writing. These children paint beautiful examples of the symbols used in Chinese writing and printing.

Covering part of one wall is a large painting, a mural, on which several children worked together. It shows a harvest scene on a commune.

The best of the Chinese children's art is shown at the National Children's Fine Arts Exhibition each year.

Elsewhere in this Children's Palace groups of children are engrossed in activities of quite a different kind. They are writing skits, rehearsing plays, and putting on puppet

(Above) Science books, fables, picture books, and tales about heroes fill the shelves of this library room in a recreation center.

(Left) A mechanical model with moving parts interests this group of young people at a Children's Palace in Shanghai.

shows. Children interested in science are observing working models at mechanical exhibits and performing chemical and electronic experiments. Another group is playing chess.

And in one of the most crowded rooms in this happy beehive of a building dozens of children are absorbed in an activity that delights children all over the world.

They are reading—a very popular hobby in China.

8

■

BOOKSTORES
&
LIBRARIES

It is Sunday afternoon in Peking. Two children, a middle school boy and his six-year-old sister, enter a large
department store and head straight for the book department on the second floor. They pass the counters where
books are being sold and go to an alcove along one wall.
This is a library.

Books for children and adults fill the shelves of the
alcove. The two children browse there, selecting the
books they will borrow to read at home.

Though this alcove library is small, it contains a variety of books. There are biographies, fast-moving action
stories, and folk tales. Like most of the Chinese movies,

ballets, and puppet shows, children's books in China combine gripping stories or interesting information with ideas about service to the country, the commune, the neighborhood.

The Chinese have set up several ways of making books available to as many people as possible. One way is to open bookstores. In towns and cities all over the country youngsters go to these stores, some of them just for children, to borrow or to buy books.

The two children in the Peking store make their choices and leave for home. The boy has picked *The Cock Crows at Midnight*, a story about peasant children who fool a greedy landlord. His other choice is *Norman Bethune in China*, the biography of a Canadian doctor who died while he was serving soldiers during the war against Japan.

The little girl is tucking into her book bag *The Monkey King Subdues the White Bone Demon*, a classic

Children and adults choose the books they will buy from the marketing group that supplies their commune in Henan.

tale, and *Lei Fang*. The latter is the story of an ordinary soldier who is famous for his kindness to other soldiers and to children. Books about him are enormously popular in China. Once, when a Lei Fang book appeared in the stores, customers snapped up the whole edition of ten thousand copies within a few hours.

In another kind of store children can find books called picture serials. These are gaudily colored paperbound books which look like American comics. Each page usually has one picture with a sentence or two to help tell the story or to give additional information. They report on scientific inventions and tell folk tales, classic stories, and true stories about China's recent history, including the war against Japan.

The picture serials are produced chiefly for two kinds of readers: older children who do not read well and adults who had no education in the past and are just now

learning to read. These readers enjoy such titles as *The
Romance of the Three Kingdoms*, another classic story;
Whistling Arrow, in which a boy catches a spy; *Tunnel
Warfare*; and *Bright Red Star*, the account of a young
man's deeds in the Revolution during the 1930s.

In the picture-serial shops the bulletin board serves
as a directory to the sixty or seventy books on hand. On it
are mounted copies of the covers of all the books available. A child looks at these covers and points to the one
he likes. The clerk then hands him a copy bearing the
same number as that on the mounted cover. The boy sits
in a chair along the wall and reads it. Sometimes a child
reads two or three picture serials in one visit to the shop.

A little girl in Nanjing learns about the soldier Lei Fang from a picture book in her nursery school.

In rural areas the back of a truck often serves as a bookstore and library. Driving out from large towns, trucks make regular stops at the farm communes in their district.

The visit of the book truck at a commune in Henan one afternoon is typical of such stops. As soon as the truck arrives, children and adults help the driver put up a table and display the books he has brought. Two eager boys look for the books they requested a few weeks earlier after hearing good accounts of them from their friends. Each boy spots the book he wants, pays for it, and leafs through other books on the table, looking at the pictures.

What kinds of books did the boys buy? A brief description of these two books shows how the writers of children's stories succeed in their two purposes: instructing and giving pleasure.

The first boy chose *In a Rainstorm*. It is a handsomely illustrated book about a soldier trying to deliver urgently

needed army supplies. A young woman weather forecaster warns him that a bad storm is on the way and advises him to wait until it is over. The soldier does not heed her advice. She alerts a nearby commune, whose members come to the soldier's aid when he runs into trouble. The supplies get through.

How many threads are woven together in this book! Here, with a suspenseful story (Will the supplies be delivered in time?), is a wealth of information about the science of weather forecasting. Here also are four ideas which the Chinese leaders want to convey:

—A woman performs work—weather forecasting—which was previously done only by men.

—Science (in this case, meteorology) is useful.

—A close bond exists between the army and the people.

—Men and women who help others are respected and honored. They are good models to follow.

The second boy's choice, *Capture the Bald Eagle*, is an adventure story. Its heroes are children who struggle up a mountain to trap the eagle that is stealing their commune's ducks. Two other popular books on the table are *Secret Bulletins*, a spy story, and *Little Ching and Hu Tzu Guard the Cornfields*, which was written especially for farm children.

China has built hundreds and hundreds of libraries. In many of them boys and girls serve as volunteers. The Shanghai libraries, for example, have over eight hundred young library helpers.

Some libraries charge a small fee for a library card. Some bookstores lend books without charge. The picture-serial stores usually charge two cents for a book or one *feng* (half a cent) for reading on the premises. Children's books cost very little. An attractive small book may sell for as little as five cents.

The large children's library in Shanghai sends out collections of books to the city's schools. Thousands of schools in China provide library books to their children.

The editors who produce books, the writers, and the artists who illustrate them are keenly interested in what kinds of books children like. They make many visits to elementary and middle schools—even to kindergartens

Mongolian girls recognize familiar characters in a picture book.

—to hear the children's opinions. The children freely discuss what they liked and didn't like about the books they have read.

The visitors listen carefully. Books that carry a moral do not have to be dry, they say, and stories that teach about duty and present good models need not be smug. It is important for the writers to learn what children find boring and what catches their interest. The artists want to know what kinds of illustrations appeal to boys and girls of different ages. These men and women note, for instance, that *Landing the Giant Sturgeon* thrills children with its elements of danger and endurance. Older children report to them that they like the Chinese translation of *Huckleberry Finn*, a great American novel. Later, when the editors, writers, and artists are producing new books, they keep the children's tastes in mind.

They seem to be succeeding. Children's libraries are busy, and bookstores are crowded. One store in Shanghai reports that it sells about 2,500 books on a normal day and as many as ten thousand on a holiday.

Parents share with their children this interest in reading. An American writer who recently returned from the People's Republic expressed amazement at their reading habits.

"The Chinese are great readers," he said. "They sit on curbs to read. They read in trains, in parks, on buses. They read standing under a street light at night. Magazines, wall newspapers, regular newspapers, books—they devour them all. It is a reading country."

For most Chinese children it is probably not easy to find a quiet, comfortable place to read at home. China is still a poor country. Houses and apartments are generally small, crowded, and not well lighted. In spite of these obstacles, children manage to read. They sit at the table or on a bed. Or, when the weather is good, they sit in the doorway or on the outside step to read.

The commune leaders encourage girls and boys to read aloud to old people who cannot read, and children find pleasure in this way of serving their neighborhood. Grandparents and elderly neighbors like to hear articles from a newspaper or an exciting war story like *Heroes of Wolf's Trap Mountain.*

Like town and city children, rural children enjoy the farm stories in *Call of the Fledgling.* They follow a little horse as he learns to face a problem in *The Foal Who Crossed the Stream.*

Books, like rallies and music, help unite the children of China. From their reading, boys and girls learn about children of other regions. Children all over China share the Monkey King's antics and Norman Bethune's heroism.

These girls of the Kazakh nationality like to read at home in the evening.

9

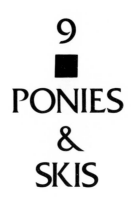

PONIES
&
SKIS

A crowd of Mongolian herders has gathered to watch a scarf contest. In this sparsely settled part of the People's Republic of China there are no sports stadiums. The herders, the long-skirted girls and women, and the young boys of their families stand on both sides of the grassy space laid out for the course. About twenty white scarfs have been spread on the grass in two long rows.

A teen-age youth on a pony gallops down the course. Leaning over as far as he can, he reaches for a scarf. The pony rushes on. The rider misses the scarf. Another rider has a turn. His hand whisks up a scarf, and he waves it in the air. Other riders follow, each one attempting to snatch up a scarf. When all the contestants have had the

These young Mongolian herders use their ponies for tending sheep and cattle, but also for recreation, as in this scarf contest.

same number of turns, each one counts his scarfs. The rider with the most scarfs is the winner.

Mongolians live in Nei Monggol (Inner Mongolia), in the northern part of China. Because the climate there is dry, few of them work as farmers. Many families earn their living tending cattle and sheep.

Though Nei Monggol is a part of China, it has its own language and customs. The Mongolians have their own ways of dressing and preparing food. The young people enjoy some of the same recreational activities that young people in cities like Canton, Shanghai, and Tianjin

Children and their families are interested spectators at this test of strength with a pole. The scene is a farm commune in Anhui Province.

like. But they have some distinctly Mongolian kinds of entertainment and sport. Their folk songs and dances are not like those in other regions of the People's Republic. Their contests on ponies are, typically, those of herders who live on high grasslands.

Mongolians are one of fifty-three nationality groups in China. Most of these minorities live in the mountainous parts of the country and in the border areas. A few live on islands off the coast. These groups differ from each other in language and ways of living. The leaders of China respect these differences, and they encourage the seventy million members of the minority groups to preserve many of their traditions.

Thus, the Muslim herders of western China continue to stage horse races, as they have for centuries. Some youths in Tibet, which is called "the roof of the world," go mountain climbing. In other regions young people practice archery and compete in wrestling matches.

Muslim boys in western China
gather for a horse race.

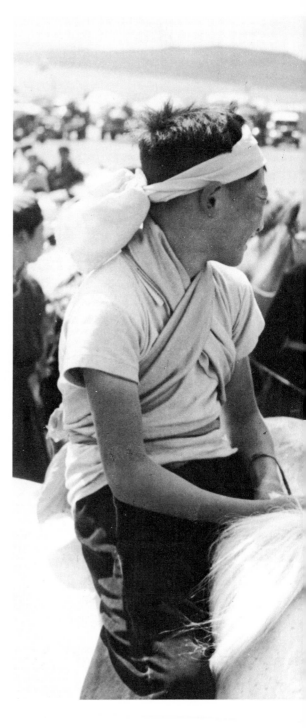

These Kazakh herdsmen tend animals on the high plains, and relax as they watch two young competitors in a wrestling match.

In the region of Xinjiang skiing is a popular sport. Bundled up in their warm, padded clothing, the youngest children troop up the easy slopes of the Altai Mountains for skiing lessons. The older boys and girls choose the more challenging ski runs higher up.

Children in the cold regions like skating, too. Just as boys and girls in Shanghai go to swimming classes, children in the colder places take lessons to improve

Young skiers in Xinjiang return from a day on the slopes of the Altai Mountains.

their skating and to learn to play ice hockey.

More than a thousand miles from the Altai ski slopes and the frozen lakes of northern China, young people belonging to minorities in the far south enjoy games that are appropriate to their climate. Instead of bundling up against the cold, they do gymnastics, jump rope, play volleyball, and watch performances under palm trees twelve months a year.

Children of workers on a construction commune in northeast China delay their skating lesson until a young friend's skates are safely fastened.

In addition to encouraging the minorities to preserve their traditions, the leaders of China help the various nationalities learn each other's dances, music, and folk tales. Thus, nursery school children in Wuhan are taught to do dances of far-off Tibet, dressed in Tibetan-style costumes. Third-graders in Fuzhou sing folk songs of the Yao people. Radio and television broadcasts and films carry songs, stories, dances, and plays from one region of China to many of the others.

Young people of the minorities also learn about each other through sports. When the National Games are

A girl of the Li minority sings a song from a Chinese opera. She and the other girls are wearing the traditional dress of their region. They live on Hainan Island in the South China Sea.

held, athletes from every region of China are brought to Peking to take part. They get to know each other when they participate in the races and other events of that big meet. Similarly, they meet one another at the cultural rallies in which singers and musicians take part.

Why do the leaders of the People's Republic think it is important to teach the young Chinese about each other's entertainments and to bring them together through sports? It is a good way, they say, to unite the fifty-three nationalities and the nine hundred million other Chinese people to make one strong country.

10

■

HOLIDAYS
&
OUTINGS

The national holidays, too, help unite the country. From north to south, from east to west, the Chinese people celebrate their major holidays in much the same way.

On October 1, Peking's broad avenues are crowded with people. They are celebrating National Day, China's most important holiday. It marks the founding of the People's Republic of China on October 1, 1949.

How do people with a great long history observe a new holiday, one that was proclaimed less than fifty years ago? Not surprisingly, they observe it with customs that have been a part of Chinese life for hundreds of years. Fireworks light up the skies. Children release pigeons and balloons into the air. They dance and sing. Families prepare festive meals. Real flowers and paper blossoms decorate parks and houses. Actors put on plays. Acrobats perform. Children play checkers and badminton.

These traditional customs remind the Chinese of their past. At the same time, new ways of celebrating express the spirit of modern China. Half a million people come to Peking from all over the country on trains, buses, and planes. They carry banners and put up posters which praise outstanding communes and urge people to help build the new China. Bands play. Leaders make speeches. Various groups march in parades and ride on floats that depict patriotic scenes.

On two other holidays, May 4 and June 1, the Chinese combine new ideas with old and new customs. The first is Youth Day. It is held in memory of the Peking students whose protests in 1919 kept the Japanese from getting possession of Shandong Province.

Families celebrating May Day at the Summer Palace in Peking watch a performance of costumed dancers.

Embroidery is an ancient Chinese art. These girls are learning to work on an embroidery frame.

The second celebrates International Children's Day. High school children direct all the activities. In parks and at Children's Palaces groups of young people give concerts, mount pageants, dance, and take part in games.

Similarly, the new joins with the old on May Day, a holiday on May 1 that honors working men and women. From all regions of China and from many different occupations, they come to Peking to parade, to watch the parades, to hear speeches, to enjoy fireworks, flowers, folk dances, and food.

New Year's Day (also called Spring Festival) is a particularly bright spot on the Chinese calendar. The date varies according to the phases of the moon. Usually, it comes near the end of January. It spreads over three days, but workers have only one day off from their jobs.

More than any other major holiday in China, New Year's is a family festival. For days in advance, children, parents, and grandparents make the traditional preparations.

There is a great bustle as they go shopping for the big
New Year's Eve dinner and for colored lanterns to
brighten the courtyard. People buy gifts for each other,
new clothes, and red paper for cut-out decorations. In
the South, house plants and flowers are a traditional kind
of decoration. Flower markets offer masses of narcissus
and flowering branches from peach and plum trees.
Many families plan holiday reunions with friends and
relatives who live in other parts of China.

On all three days of the New Year celebration the

A group of friends spend the day together in a park.

stores are crowded with merrymakers who buy toys, kites, and books. Parents stop at outdoor stalls to treat their children to holiday snacks like tangerines, cakes, and candy.

New Year's is a time for seeing *wushu*, plays, and new films. Dragons, which often appear in old Chinese painting, sculpture, and literature, appear also on New Year's Day. Acrobats and dancers in dragon costumes give performances accompanied by drums and volleys of firecracker explosions. Other entertainers, dressed as bizarre lions, perform a special kind of *wushu*.

From China's past have come many of the ways young people amuse themselves at home and on outings with their families and friends. By themselves or with two or three playmates, they walk on stilts and play marbles, hopscotch, and leapfrog. Card games, checkers, and chess are favorite pastimes in the house and outdoors all over China.

On days when the wind is right, children fly kites. And what beautiful kites they are! Made of silk or paper, they are designed and painted to look like fanciful butterflies, birds, dragons, and frogs.

The youngest children play with dolls, toy cars and airplanes, and folk toys in the shapes of tigers, cats, and dragons. Some boys and girls catch crickets and keep them in small bamboo cages as pets. Others keep goldfish and canaries. In most parts of China children do not have large pets. Fujian Province and Tibet are two exceptions. In those areas many households include a dog or a cat.

Girls of several nationality groups collect insects and plant specimens at a scientific summer camp in Yunnan Province.

Girls, especially among the national minorities, like to embroider. They work traditional flower and dragon designs on skirts, blouses, and hats.

Boys in rural areas combine the fun of hunting and fishing with the satisfaction of bringing home a river goldfish, a bird, or a rabbit for the family's dinner.

Tourists who visit China notice that almost all of these amusements are familiar to children in the United States and Europe. So they are not surprised to see Chinese children playing blindman's buff and the bouncing ball game that American children call "One, Two, Three O'Leary."

Pupils from elementary and middle schools in Tibet have their first look at the sea.

Right along with these old games and hobbies, Chinese boys and girls enjoy newer pastimes like roller skating, stamp collecting, picture taking, and bicycle riding. The newest activity, known chiefly to city children, is Frisbee tossing.

Children now do what only a few fortunate Chinese did before the Revolution. With families or friends, they take short trips and go on outings to parks. They attend sports events and day camps. They visit historical places and interesting sites like the Great Wall.

Not until a generation ago could the ordinary Chinese people enter the Forbidden City, which is sometimes

A crowd filled the Peking Workers Stadium in September, 1977, to watch the Chinese national soccer team play the New York Cosmos. The first game ended in a tie. The Chinese won the second game.

called the Palace Museum. Only the rulers and their families, guests, workmen, and servants were allowed through the gates.

Now it is a public park open to everyone. Here, visitors walk through arches and marble gates, past red and gold pillars and golden-roofed palaces. It is like a storybook tale coming true in front of their eyes. But this is—or was—a real royal city. Thrones, jade statues, and carved dragons and lions recall the emperor who had this huge royal residence built five hundred years ago. Signs remind them of another side of this past. "All this was built

Children and their parents sometimes take short trips to historical places. This is the entrance to an empress's tomb at the Eastern Ching burial sites.

Three Chinese girls and a group of visiting American basketball players examine a jar at the Ming Tombs.

in the time of bitterness," the signs say. "It was created through the efforts of people like you."

Another former royal residence, the Summer Palace outside Peking, delights families on a short excursion. They stroll on its covered walks, visit its elegant buildings, and take a boat ride on the lake.

Like the royal palaces, museums attract hundreds of parents and children on outings. Peking's museums offer them a wide choice. A family interested in early man will

Young girls on an outing to the Forbidden City rush to greet
American tourists.

plan an afternoon at the Historical Museum. Along with
early earthenware and models of prehistoric cave dwell-
ings, it displays a wax model of Peking man. He lived in
China about 500,000 years ago.

If a family likes to learn about the arts and crafts of
minority people, its choice will be the Minorities Cultural Palace Museum. There it will find colorful clothing,
jewelry, and pottery from China's many nationalities.

Perhaps an elderly member of a family has described
some of the moving events he remembers from his

133

A little boy and his grandparents attend a sculpture exhibit at their commune near Tianjin. The painted figures represent various occupations.

Two students are enjoying an afternoon together.

Boys and girls at a summer day camp amuse themselves on a beach.

experiences in the Revolution. That may have stirred the children's interest in a trip to the Museum of the Revolution. Among its exhibits are maps of the route taken on the Long March and tableaux of Mao Zedong's life.

Art exhibitions draw many families on their free days, not only in Peking but also in towns and small cities.

Hundreds of visitors every day are attracted to the Forbidden City, or Palace Museum, in Peking.

Children with an interest in science and technology find much to enjoy and much to learn at the Children's Railway in a Harbin park and at the model power plant and the Clock Museum in Peking. In Nanjing they can see one of China's most famous engineering achievements, the bridge over the Yangtse River. There, too, they can climb a hill overlooking the city to visit an astronomy observatory.

For Chinese families, as for families everywhere, a trip

These boys are waiting for a puppet show to begin. It is being performed in a park near their home.

to a zoo is a happy occasion. Adding to the fun are the stops at teahouses for refreshments and the popsicles and fried crullers consumed along the way.

The people of China have seen, and are still seeing, many important changes in their lives. Amid all these changes—changes in their ways of working, of thinking, of enjoying themselves—one thing has not changed: the pattern of family life. As it has been from ages past, the

An old man spends a pleasant hour with his grandchildren.

Chinese family remains a close-knit, stable unit. Parents, children, grandparents, and perhaps another relative, usually live together in the same house or apartment or have homes near each other. They divide the responsibilities and share the joys of family living.

Thus it can happen that after the excitements of a puppet show, a Ping-Pong game, a *wushu* lesson, or a day at the beach with friends, boys and girls find a special pleasure in just sitting on a bench with a parent, an uncle, a grandfather.

GLOSSARY

Spelling adopted January 1, 1979	Spelling used before 1979
Altai	Altai
Anhui	Anhwei
Beidaihe	Beidaihe
Beijing	Peking
biba	pipa
Chang Jiang	Yangtse
dai ji-quan	tai chi-chuan
Deng Xiaoping	Teng Hsiao-p'ing
erhu	erhu
feng	feng
Fujian	Fukien
Fuzhou	Foochow
galong jin	galong jin
gong-fu	kung-fu
gujin	gujin

Guangdong	Kwangtung
Gwangzhou	Canton
Hainan	Hainan
Harbin	Harbin
Henan	Honan
Jinan	Tsinan
Kazakh	Kazakh
Mao Zedong	Mao Tse-tung
Nanjing	Nanking
Nei Monggol	Inner Mongolia
Shanghai	Shanghai
Shandong	Shantung
sheng	sheng
Sichuan	Szechwan
Tadzhik	Tadzhik
Tianjin	Tientsin
Wuhan	Wuhan
wushu	wushu
Xinjiang	Sinkiang
Xizang	Tibet
Yao	Yao
Yunnan	Yunnan

The letter "x" in the new spelling is pronounced like "sh" in the English word "shop."

Following the usage adopted by *The New York Times*, this book uses the old spellings of Peking, Tibet, Canton, Inner Mongolia, and Yangtse River.

INDEX

Picture Credits

Children's Palace, Shanghai, 21 (bottom), 81, 82, 84–85, 89, 90, 92, 94, 95

Foreign Language Press, 23, 31

Allyn Rickett, 21 (top)

The United Methodist Church, Board of Global Ministries, 71, 72, 86, 93, 127, 137, 138

Isobel Willcox, 26, 33 (right), 101

Xinhua News Agency, courtesy of U.S.-China People's Friendship Association, 2–3, 4–5, 7, 8, 10–11, 14–15, 17, 18, 19, 24–25, 27, 28, 32–33, 35, 36, 37, 38, 39, 41, 42–43, 44, 46, 47, 48–49, 50, 54–55, 57, 58, 59, 60, 62–63, 64–65, 67, 68–69, 73, 74, 76–77, 79, 87, 99, 104, 108–109, 111, 112, 114–115, 116, 117, 118, 119, 122–123, 125, 128, 129, 130, 131, 132, 133, 134 (top and bottom), 135, 136

Map on pages xiv-xv is by Dyno Lowenstein